To all children in the world and to everyone that seek to know God for themselves...

Copyright © 2022 by Ugochi Gift Agbontain
All rights reserved. No part of this publication may be reproduced in whole or in part, or stored in a retrieval system, or transmitted in any form or by any means, electronic, mechanical, photocopying, recording, or otherwise, without the permission of the publisher, except as provided by United States of America copyright law.

HOW TO READ THESE BIBLE STORIES

The stories can be read aloud to each child or to a group of children by an adult.

Each message in the story should be well illustrated to the child

Declare the prayers in each story openly over the child, or have the child/children declare aloud together the prayers in each story as the verse of the day for mediation

BIBLE BABIES

Stories retold by Ugochi Gift Agbontain
Illustrated by Tuly Akter

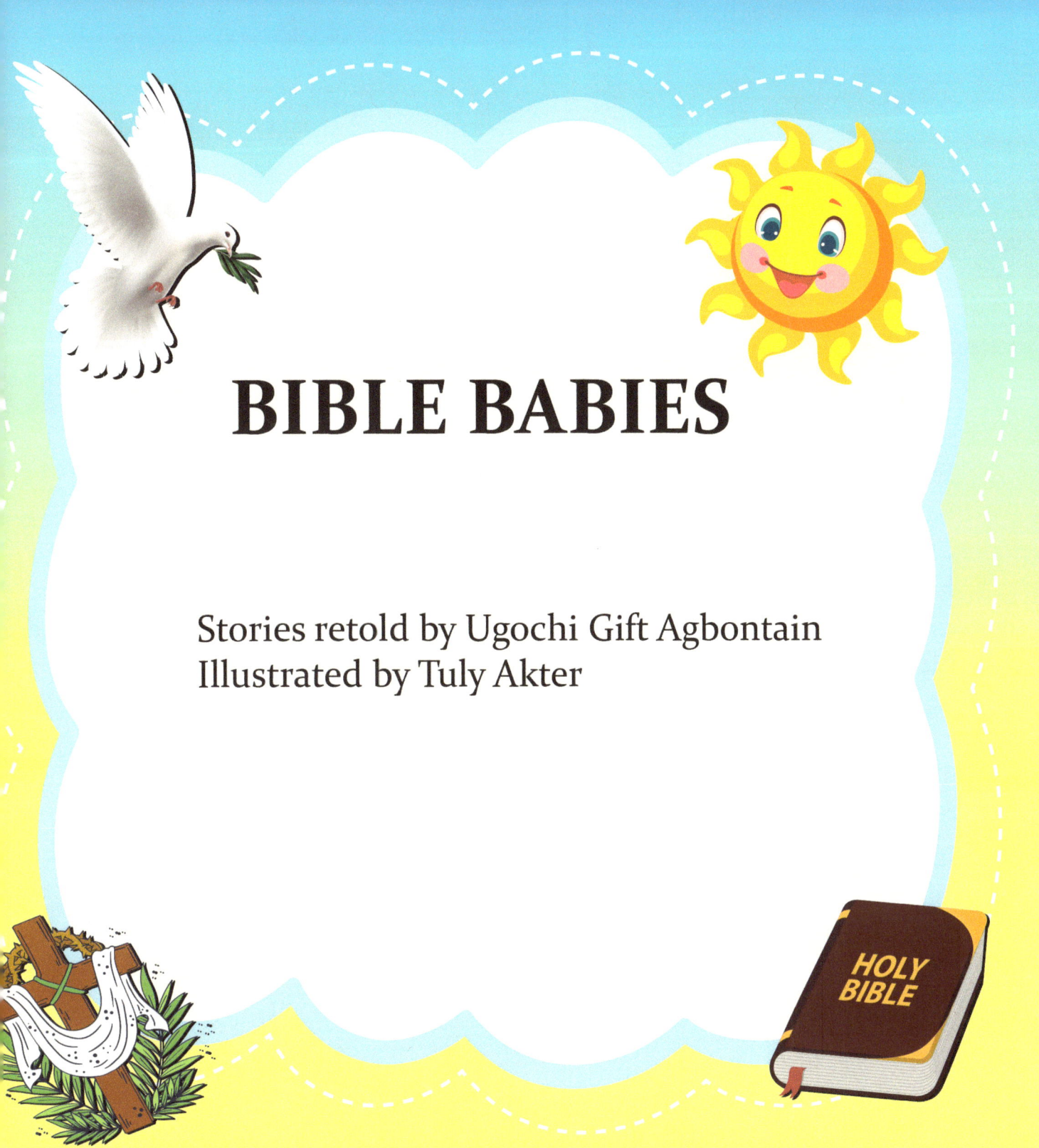

BABY JESUS
Matthew 1:18-25, Matthew 2:1-12

Once upon a time, there was a woman named Mary, who was a virgin. She was hoping to be married soon, to a man named Joseph. But before they were married, she found out she was going to have a baby by the Holy Spirit.

Joseph, was worried as he slept while he was thinking, about how to break his engagement plans with Mary, when an angel of the Lord appeared to him in a dream and told him to take Mary as his wife, because she was conceived by the Holy Spirit.

The angel of the Lord, instructed Joseph to name the baby JESUS as soon as he is born; because, he was going to save his people from their sins.
When Joseph woke up, he did according to the angel's instructions and took Mary in as his wife.

Not too long, Mary gave birth to a baby and they named him "JESUS". Jesus was born in the town of Bethlehem in Judea, at the time when Herod was king. Mary, the mother of Jesus gave birth to him in a Manger, because there was no room for her to stay in the inn.

Jesus was born with a purpose, which was to save the world from their sins.

Soon afterwards, wise men came to see Jesus, bringing with them; gold, frankincense and myrrh. They knelt down and worshipped, as they presented their gifts to Baby Jesus. And Jesus continued to grow in wisdom, stature and favor with God and Men.

Action/Prayer: *I declare, I was born with a purpose. And so, I will fulfill my purpose as Jesus, as I grow in wisdom, stature and favor with God and Men. Amen*

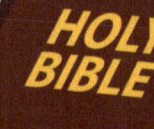

BABY MOSES
Exodus 2:1-10; 6:20

Once upon a time, there was a woman named Jochebed. Who gave birth to a baby named "Moses," in the land of Egypt. At that time, the king of Egypt demanded that all Israelites male babies should be slain, as soon as they were born.

However, Moses' mother, Jochebed decided not to slay her baby, because she saw he was a special and goodly child. Instead, she hid baby Moses in a basket and place it besides the river bank.

Baby Moses was born with a purpose to save the children of Israel from slavery and from the land of Egypt.

Soon afterwards, the king's daughter came to the river to have her bath. There, she spotted baby Moses in a basket by the river bank. She immediately had compassion on him and decided to take Moses in for a son, even though she knew he was a Hebrew child.

So, Moses became a prince as he continued to grow in the king's palace. He knew his origin, and always looked for opportunities to help his people – Israel.

Action/Prayer: I am special, unique and favored just like baby Moses, and I always look for opportunities to help people.

BABY SAMUEL
I Samuel 1:1-18, 20, 24-28

Once upon a time, there was a woman named Hannah.
She was married to a man named, Elkanah.
Elkanah, loved Hannah so much even though she could not bear him a son, because she was barren.

One day, Hannah prayed unto God.
She cried so loudly without uttering a word, as she prayed to God for a baby in the Temple, and promised, to dedicate the baby to God all his life, if her request is granted by God.

Right there in the Temple, came Prophet Eli, who declared to Hannah that her request for a baby has been granted by God.
Hannah went home happily, and was never worried again.

Not too long, she became pregnant and gave birth to a son whom she named, "Samuel".

Hannah went back to the Temple and gave Baby Samuel to the Lord. Samuel, served in the house of the Lord under the Prophet Eli.

Later, Samuel grew up and became a great prophet in Israel. There was no prophet in Israel like Samuel.

And he continued to grow in the service of the Lord.

Action/Prayer: *God will answer my request just like Hannah, as I continue to be great, just like Samuel.*

BABY SAMSON

Judges 13:1-5, 24-25

Once upon a time, there was a people named – "Israel", who sinned against the Lord. Because of this, God permitted a people called the "Philistines", to rule over them for forty years.

One day, the Lord's angel appeared to a woman, who had never had a child. And was married to a man named, Manoah from the town of Zorah. The angel, told her that she will soon be pregnant with a son. He instructed her, never to drink any wine or even eat forbidden foods, and never to cut the son's hair after he was born.

The son was to be dedicated to God as a Nazirite and his purpose was to save the children of Israel from the Philistines.

Soon afterwards, the woman gave birth to a son and named him "Samson".
Baby Samson, grew up and became so strong and bold.

The hand of God rested on Samson.
He was so strong, that he could tear a lion apart with his bare hands.
He even slayed a thousand Philistines only with a donkey's jawbone

The Philistines, always looked for ways to punish the Israelites.
And, everyone in Israel dreaded the Philistines, except Samson as God used him greatly to slew many of the Philistines.

Action/Prayer: I have been dedicated to God for an assignment, and I am strong and bold just like Samson

BABY JOHN

Luke 1:5-25, 57-66

Once upon a time, there was a woman named Elizabeth, who was married to a man named Zachariah.
And both of them, served continually in the house of the Lord.
Elizabeth never had a child for Zachariah, because she was barren.
One day, an angel of the Lord named Gabriel, appeared to Zachariah while he was serving in the Temple.
Angel Gabriel, declared to Zachariah that he was going to be a father soon.
He told him, his wife, Elizabeth will soon be pregnant;
And he was to name the child "John".

Angel Gabriel, told Zachariah that the child would be a Nazirite and was going to be filled with the Holy Spirit.
His purpose, was to bring back many of the people of Israel to the Lord. In doubt, Zachariah, questioned the angel because he felt he was very old. And so, became deaf as declared by Angel Gabriel.

Sometime later, Elizabeth became pregnant.
And not too long, she delivered the baby and he was called "John". Everyone was filled with surprise, as they rejoiced with them and Zachariah was able to speak again.

Baby John grew and became a great prophet in Israel.
He was chosen to be the forerunner of Jesus.
His garment was made of Camel's hair and he lived in the desert. His food was locust and wild honey.
And he preached about the coming of the Messiah – Jesus!
As he baptized everyone that repented from their sins.

Everyone in Israel had great regard and respect for John the Baptist. And he was great even in the Lord's sight.
As the Lord's power was always upon him.

Action/Prayer: I am filled with the power of the Holy Spirit, as I have been forgiven from my sins.

BABY ISAAC

Genesis 17:1-21; 21:1-8

Once upon a time, there was a woman named Sarai, who was married to a man named Abram.
Both of them, never had a child and were very old.

One day, the Lord appeared to Abram when he was ninety-nine years old, and made an everlasting covenant with him. He promised to give him many descendants, and also changed his name from Abram to Abraham, and that of his wife from Sarai to Sarah.

Abraham laughed within himself...
He couldn't imagine he could have a son at that old age, but he dared to believe God's promise.
And God honored him by fulfilling His promise.

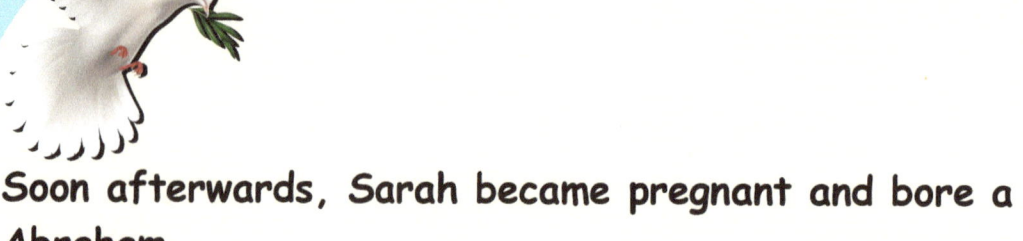

Soon afterwards, Sarah became pregnant and bore a son to Abraham.

He named the child "Isaac", because he believed God has brought him joy and laughter even in his old age.

Abraham, was a hundred years old when Baby Isaac was born, while Sarah was ninety years old too.

And Isaac continued to grow and was loved by everyone.

Action/Prayer: I will trust in you oh Lord, even when the odds are against me just like Abraham, because I know you keep your promises.

BABY ESAU & JACOB

Genesis 25:21-26

Once upon a time, there was a man named Isaac.
He was the son of Abraham, and was married to a woman named, Rebecca.
Rebecca, never had a child for Isaac after they were married.

One day, Isaac prayed to the Lord for his wife Rebecca.
He asked God to bless them with a child and God answered his prayers.
Sometime later, Rebecca became pregnant...
She was going to have twins. But before they were born, they struggled against each other in her womb.
Rebecca was so worried and she went to inquire of the Lord.

God told Rebecca that two nations are within her;
That the older one will serve the younger one.

Not too long, Rebecca gave birth to the twins.
The first was named Esau; He came out reddish and hairy.
The second one was named Jacob; He was born holding tightly to the heel of Esau.

Isaac was sixty years old when they were born.
Rebecca was excited about their babies and they blessed the name of the Lord.

Action/Prayer: I will ask the Lord for what I need, for he will surely grant my request just like Isaac

BABY JOSEPH

Genesis 30:1, 22-24

Once upon a time, there was a man named Jacob;
Who had two wives - Leah and Rachel by name.
But, Jacob loved Rachel so much more than Leah.
He had worked in the fields of Laban, Rachel's dad for fourteen years just to have her for a wife.

However, Racheal was sad because she couldn't have a child for Jacob.
She would cry all night to her husband to give her a child.
She did everything she could, but was still unable to bear her own child for Jacob.

One day, God remembered Rachel...
He answered her prayer, and made it possible for her to have children.
Rachel became pregnant and gave birth to a son.
She named the son "Joseph", because she believed God has taken away her disgrace by giving her a son.

She was never sad again and she loved Baby Joseph all her life.

Action/Prayer: God has decided to favor me, because He has remembered me.

BABY SOLOMON

2 Samuel 12:24-25

Once upon a time, there was a woman named Bathsheba, who was married to a king named, David.

She lost her previous baby and cried all night because she was very sad.

Nevertheless, her husband, King David comforted her and told her everything will be alright.

Soon afterwards, she conceived and bore a son.

The child was named "Solomon" by his father, David the king.

The Lord loved Baby Solomon so much, and even commanded a prophet named, Nathan to give him a special name.

Prophet Nathan obeyed the Lord's instruction and went to visit Baby Solomon.
He named Baby Solomon "Jedidiah", because the Lord loved him so much.

Baby Solomon continued to grow in the palace as one of King David sons. He became the wisest man on earth, and was loved by everyone around him.

Action/Prayer: I declare that I am loved by God and by everyone around me

BABY OBED
Ruth 4:13-17

Once upon a time, there was a woman named Ruth, a Moabite. She was a daughter-in-law to Naomi, an Israelite.
Naomi, had lost her husband and sons in the country of Moab, during a time of hardship in Israel.

About this time, Naomi decided to return back to Bethlehem in Judah, where she previously lived.
But Ruth, Naomi's daughter-in-law couldn't allow her to go back alone.
She made up her mind to follow her mother-in-law Naomi, even though she was a Moabite and never had a child for her.

Not long ago, when they got to Jerusalem, Ruth, the daughter-in-law of Naomi, found favor in the eyes of a wealthy man named, Boaz.

Boaz fell in love with Ruth and decided to take her in for a wife.

The Lord blessed Ruth and gave her a son whom was named, "Obed".

Everyone that knew Naomi, Ruth's mother-in-law was happy, and they rejoiced with her because, they believed the son has brought new life to her after all the pains she had been through, and will give her security in her old age.

Baby Obed continued to grow as he became the father of Jesse, whom then became the father of King David.

Action/Prayer: I declare I have the favor of God like Ruth and I am completely secured through the blood of Jesus.

www.ingramcontent.com/pod-product-compliance
Lightning Source LLC
Chambersburg PA
CBHW040723060526

44119CB00083B/305